FAVORITE BASEBALL ★ TEAMS ★

NEW YORK YANKEES

BY K.C. KELLEY

The
Child's
World®

Published by The Child's World®
1980 Lookout Drive • Mankato, MN 56003-1705
800-599-READ • www.childsworld.com

ACKNOWLEDGMENTS
The Child's World®: Mary Berendes,
        Publishing Director
The Design Lab: Kathleen Petelinsek, Design
Shoreline Publishing Group, LLC: James
        Buckley Jr., Production Director

PHOTOS
Cover: Getty Images
Interior: All photos by Focus on Baseball except:
AP/Wide World: 5, 17, 26 (inset); Baseball Hall of
Fame: 9, 22; Getty: 18

LIBRARY OF CONGRESS
CATALOGING-IN-PUBLICATION DATA
Kelley, K. C.
  New York Yankees / by K.C. Kelley.
     p. cm. — (Favorite baseball teams)
  Includes index.
  ISBN 978-1-60253-380-6 (library bound : alk. paper)
  1. New York Yankees (Baseball team)—History—
Juvenile literature. I. Title. II. Series.
  GV875.N4K45 2010
  796.357'64097471—dc22   2009039451

Printed in the United States of America
Mankato, Minnesota
September 2010
PA02076

On the cover: Derek Jeter,
Shortstop

CONTENTS

Go, Yankees!

Every baseball team wants to win the **World Series**. No team has won more of them than the New York Yankees! This famous club has won 27 World Series. That's more than twice as many as any other team. Actually, the Yankees are the most successful **professional** sports team in America. No other team has won its sport's championship more than the Yankees. Let's meet this amazing team of champions!

Derek Jeter (right) and the Yankees celebrate a big win during the 2009 season. ▶

Who Are the Yankees?

The New York Yankees are a team in baseball's American League (A.L.). The A.L. joins with the National League to form Major League Baseball. The Yankees play in the East Division of the A.L. The division winners get to play in the league playoffs. The playoff winners from the two leagues face off in the World Series. The Yankees have won 27 World Series championships, more than any other team.

◀ In a game against the Minnesota Twins, Derek Jeter is ready to make a catch at second base.

Where They Came From

In 1903, a team called the Baltimore Orioles moved to New York City. The team changed its name to the New York Highlanders. They became the Yankees in 1913. They didn't do very well for their first 20 years. Then a super player named Babe Ruth came along. He helped them become baseball's best.

The great Babe Ruth whacked 714 home runs in his career. He stopped playing in 1935, but only two players since then have hit more homers. ▶

Who They Play

The New York Yankees play 162 games each season. That includes 18 games against the other teams in their division, the A.L. East. The Yankees have won 16 A.L. East championships. The other East teams are the Baltimore Orioles, the Boston Red Sox, the Tampa Bay Rays, and the Toronto Blue Jays. New York has a big **rivalry** with Boston. Those two teams always have great battles. The Yankees also play some teams from the National League. Their N.L. **opponents** change every year.

◀ Crunch! Another action-packed game between the Red Sox (sliding) and the Yankees (flying!).

Where They Play

A new Yankee Stadium opened in 2009. It's a huge ballpark that can hold more than 50,000 people. It has a Yankees Museum and miles of walkways. Fans can find food from many countries at stands in the ballpark. The Yankees' old home, also called Yankee Stadium, was the first ballpark to have three levels of seats. New or old, Yankee Stadium is one of baseball's most famous homes.

This is the main entrance to the new Yankee Stadium in New York City. ▶

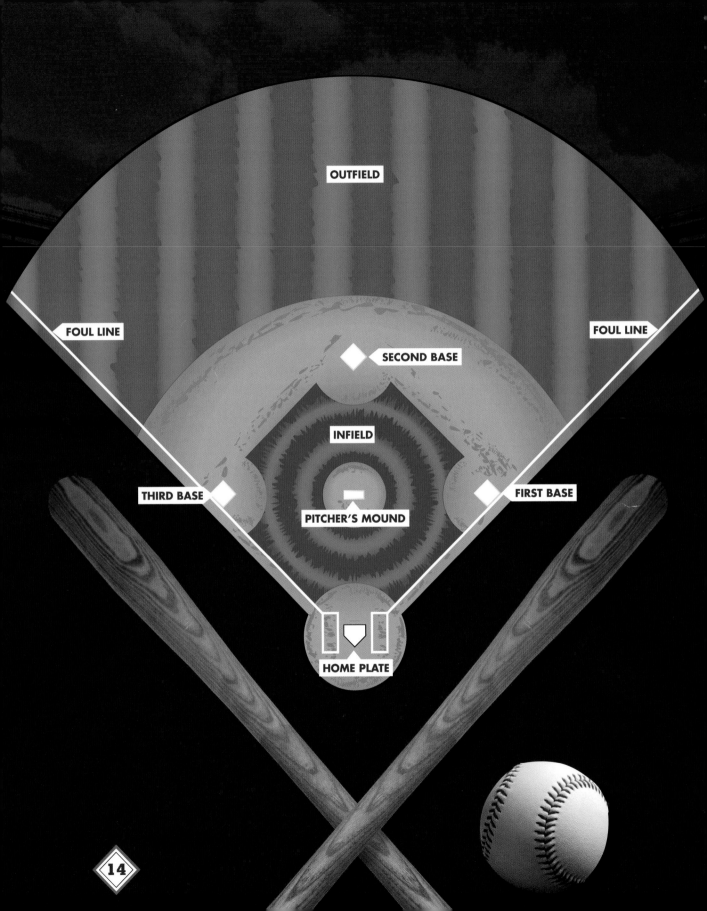

OUTFIELD

FOUL LINE

FOUL LINE

SECOND BASE

INFIELD

THIRD BASE

FIRST BASE

PITCHER'S MOUND

HOME PLATE

14

The Baseball Diamond

Baseball games are played on a diamond. Four bases form this diamond shape. The bases are 90 feet (27 m) apart. The area around the bases is called the **infield**. At the center of the infield is the pitcher's mound. The grass area beyond the bases is called the **outfield**. White lines start at **home plate** and go toward the outfield. These are the foul lines. Baseballs hit outside these lines are out of play. The outfield walls are about 300-450 feet (91-137 m) from home plate.

Big Days!

The Yankees have had so many great seasons, it's hard to pick just a few. But these are some of the best:

1927: Some experts call this the best baseball team of all time. The Yankees pounded the other A.L. teams. Then they won the World Series in four straight games.

1953: This season's Yankees were baseball powerhouses. They won their fifth straight World Series! No other team has even won three straight.

2000: The Yankees played the Mets in a "Subway Series" between two New York teams. The Yankees won a thrilling World Series played all in one city!

2009: The Yankees move into a new Yankee Stadium . . . and win another World Series. Their victory over the Philadelphia Phillies gives them 27 championships in all!

Mariano Rivera holds up the 2009 World Series trophy as his teammates cheer! ▶

Tough Days!

The Yankees don't have many bad seasons. They've been one of baseball's best teams for a long time. But they can't always win! Here are some of their not-so-good years:

1908: This team lost more games than any in Yankee history—103!

1966: Just two years before, they were in the World Series. But this year, the team finished last in the A.L. It was their lowest finish since 1912!

1990: This was a tough time for Yankees' fans. The team lost 95 games and finished last in the A.L. East.

◀ Longtime Yankees owner George Steinbrenner wasn't happy when the Yankees played poorly in 1990.

Meet the Fans

Yankees fans are very **loyal**. Even when they move away from New York City, they support their team. When the team plays in other cities, its fans are there to cheer, too! Yankees' fans are used to winning. They expect their team to do well. And they're not afraid to let the players know when they're not working hard enough! Win or lose, Yankees fans love their team.

The numbers on the wall above the fans are "retired." They were worn ▶ by Yankees greats, but will never be worn again.

Heroes Then . . .

The Yankees have seen a parade of superstars over the years. Here are just a few. Babe Ruth and Lou Gehrig are two of the best players of all time. They played for the Yankees in the 1920s and 1930s. Ruth still holds many batting records. Gehrig had 13 seasons with 100 or more runs batted in (RBI). Outfielder Joe DiMaggio was a Yankees star in the 1930s and 1940s. He was known for his smooth playing style. In the 1950s, outfielder Mickey Mantle and catcher Yogi Berra led the Yankees to more championships. Berra won three **Most Valuable Player (MVP)** Awards. In the 1970s, pitcher Ron Guidry and slugger Reggie Jackson were Yankees stars.

◄ Babe Ruth and Lou Gehrig were two of the most powerful sluggers in baseball history.

Heroes Now . . .

Shortstop Derek Jeter has been a star since he was the **Rookie of the Year** in 1996. He has helped the Yankees reach the playoffs 13 times! First baseman Mark Teixiera joined the team in 2009. He's a powerful batter. Second baseman Robinson Cano has speed and a solid bat. At third base, Alex Rodriguez might be one of the best players of all time. **Relief pitcher** Mariano Rivera is one of the best ever as a "closer." He comes in at the end of games to "close out" the other team.

Derek Jeter, Shortstop

Mark Teixiera, First Base

Mariano Rivera, Pitcher

BATTING HELMET

TEAM JERSEY

BATTING GLOVE

BAT

TEAM PANTS

CATCHER'S MASK

CATCHER'S CHEST PROTECTOR

CATCHER'S MITT

CATCHER'S SHIN GUARD

BASEBALL CLEATS

Jorge Posada, Catcher

Gearing Up

Baseball players all wear a team jersey and pants. They have to wear a team hat in the field and a helmet when batting. Take a look at Robinson Cano and Jorge Posada to see some other parts of a baseball player's uniform.

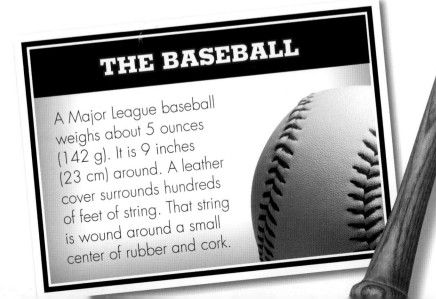

THE BASEBALL

A Major League baseball weighs about 5 ounces (142 g). It is 9 inches (23 cm) around. A leather cover surrounds hundreds of feet of string. That string is wound around a small center of rubber and cork.

SPORTS STATS

Here are some all-time career records for the New York Yankees. All the stats are through the 2009 season.

HOME RUNS

Babe Ruth, 659
Mickey Mantle, 536

RUNS BATTED IN

Lou Gehrig, 1,995
Babe Ruth, 1,975

BATTING AVERAGE

Babe Ruth, .349
Lou Gehrig, .340

WINS BY A PITCHER

Whitey Ford, 236
Red Ruffing, 231

STOLEN BASES

Rickey Henderson, 326
Derek Jeter, 305

WINS BY A MANAGER

Joe McCarthy, 1,460

EARNED RUN AVERAGE

Rich Gossage, 2.14
Mariano Rivera, 2.25

Glossary

home plate a five-sided rubber pad where batters stand to swing, and where runners touch base to score runs

infield the area around and between the four bases of a baseball diamond

loyal supporting something no matter what

manager the person who is in charge of the team and chooses who will bat and pitch

Most Valuable Player (MVP) a yearly award given to the top player in each league

opponents teams or players that play against each other

outfield the large, grass area beyond the infield of a baseball diamond

professional a professional is someone who gets paid to play a sport

relief pitcher a pitcher who comes into a game to take another pitcher's place

rivalry an ongoing competition between teams that play each other often, over a long time

Rookie of the Year an award given to the top first-year player in each league

World Series the Major League Baseball championship, played each year between the winners of the American and National Leagues

Find Out More

BOOKS

Buckley, James Jr. *Eyewitness Baseball*. New York: DK Publishing, 2010.

Roth, B. A. *Derek Jeter: A Yankee Hero*. New York: Grosset & Dunlap, 2009.

Stewart, Mark. *New York Yankees*. Chicago: Norwood House Press, 2007.

Teitelbaum, Michael. *Baseball*. Ann Arbor, MI: Cherry Lake Publishing, 2009.

WEB SITES

Visit our Web page for links about the New York Yankees and other pro baseball teams.

childsworld.com/links

Note to Parents, Teachers, and Librarians: We routinely verify our Web links to make sure they are safe, active sites—so encourage your readers to check them out!

Index

ABOUT THE AUTHOR

K.C. Kelley has written dozens of books on baseball and other sports for young readers. He has also been a youth baseball coach and called baseball games on the radio. His favorite team? The Boston Red Sox.